Bugs, Bugs, Bugs!

Moths

by Fran Howard

Consulting Editor: Gail Saunders-Smith, PhD

Consultant: Gary A. Dunn, MS, Director of Education
Young Entomologists' Society Inc.
Lansing, Michigan

Capstone
press

Mankato, Minnesota

Pebble Plus is published by Capstone Press,
151 Good Counsel Drive, P.O. Box 669, Mankato, Minnesota 56002.
www.capstonepress.com

1 2 3 4 5 6 10 09 08 07 06 05

Library of Congress Cataloging-in-Publication Data
Howard, Fran, 1953–
     Moths / by Fran Howard.
     p. cm.—(Pebble plus: bugs, bugs, bugs!)
     Includes bibliographical references and index.
     ISBN 0-7368-3644-6 (hardcover)
     1. Moths—Juvenile literature. I. Title. II. Series.
QL644.2.H68 2005
595.78—dc22   2004011971

Summary: Simple text and photographs describe the physical characteristics of moths.

Editorial Credits
Sarah L. Schuette, editor; Linda Clavel, set designer; Kate Opseth, book designer; Kelly Garvin,
     photo researcher; Scott Thoms, photo editor

Photo Credits
Ann & Rob Simpson, 17
Bruce Coleman Inc./IFA, 6–7; Kjell Sandved, 5; Mik Dakin, 15
Dwight R. Kuhn, cover
Image Ideas, 1
Kevin Barry, 9
Minden Pictures/Mitsuhiko Imamori, 18–19; Tim Fitzharris, 20–21
Photodisc, back cover
Robert McCaw, 11, 12–13

2/06

Note to Parents and Teachers

The Bugs, Bugs, Bugs! set supports national science standards related to the diversity of
life and heredity. This book describes and illustrates moths. The images support
early readers in understanding the text. The repetition of words and phrases helps early
readers learn new words. This book also introduces early readers to subject-specific
vocabulary words, which are defined in the Glossary section. Early readers may need
assistance to read some words and to use the Table of Contents, Glossary, Read More,
Internet Sites, and Index sections of the book.

Table of Contents

What Are Moths?

Moths are insects
with large wings
and fat bodies.

How Moths Look

Some moths are colorful.

Other moths have dull wings.

Moths have six legs.
They crawl on leaves
and plants.

Many moths are about

the size of a dime.

Moths have two antennas.
Moths use antennas
to feel and smell.

What Moths Do

Many moths fly at night.
They try to stay away
from bats. Bats eat moths.

Moths hide from other animals during the day.

Moths stay safe
by sitting on leaves.
Moths rest with
their wings down.

Some moths scare other
animals with their eyespots.
These spots look like
the eyes of a bigger animal.

Glossary

antenna—a feeler; insects use antennas to sense movement, to smell, and to listen to each other.

dull—not colorful

eyespots—the spots on an insect's wings that look like the eyes of a bigger animal; eyespots can be different sizes and colors.

insect—a small animal with a hard outer shell, six legs, three body sections, and two antennas; most insects have wings.

Read More

Farndon, John. *Butterflies and Moths.* In Touch with Nature. San Diego: Blackbirch Press, 2004.

Frost, Helen. *Moths.* Insects. Mankato, Minn.: Pebble Books, 2001.

Loewen, Nancy. *Night Fliers: Moths in Your Backyard.* Backyard Bugs. Minneapolis: Picture Window Books, 2004.

Internet Sites

FactHound offers a safe, fun way to find Internet sites related to this book. All of the sites on FactHound have been researched by our staff.

Here's how:

1. Visit *www.facthound.com*

2. Type in this special code **0736836446** for age-appropriate sites. Or enter a search word related to this book for a more general search.

3. Click on the **Fetch It** button.

FactHound will fetch the best sites for you!

Index

Word Count: 102
Grade: 1
Early-Intervention Level: 10